Ice Dancing

BY CLAIRE THROP

Consultant: Kristin Eberth
United States Figure Skating double gold medalist
Professional figure skater with Disney On Ice

CAPSTONE PRESS
a capstone imprint

Snap Books are published by Capstone Press,
1710 Roe Crest Drive, North Mankato, Minnesota 56003
www.mycapstone.com

Library of Congress Cataloging-in-Publication Data
Names: Throp, Claire.
Title: Ice dancing / by Claire Throp.
Description: North Mankato, Minnesota : Capstone Press, [2018] |
Series:
   Figure skating. Snap books | Includes bibliographical references
   and index.
Identifiers: LCCN 2017009664
ISBN 9781515781851 (library binding)
ISBN 9781515781899 (eBook PDF)
Subjects: LCSH: Ice dancing—Juvenile literature.
Classification: LCC GV850.45 .T47 2018 | DDC 796.91/2—dc23
LC record available at https://lccn.loc.gov/2017009664

Editorial Credits
Brenda Haugen, editor; Veronica Scott, designer; Kelli Lageson,
media researcher; Kathy McColley, production specialist

Photo Credits
Alamy: ITAR-TASS Photo Agency, 25, PA Images, 17, REUTERS/Jerry
Lampen, 16; Getty Images: Corbis/Eddy Lemaistre, 20, Hero Images,
18, JedJacobsohn, 28, The Asahi Shimbun, 29; Newscom: EPA/ANJA
NIEDRINGHAUS, 24, EPA/TANNEN MAURY, 13, ZUMAPRESS/
CanWest, 11; Shutterstock: Aija Lehtonen, 14, anfisa focusova, 3,
CREATISTA, 8, Diego Barbieri, 5, Lilyana Vynogradova, 27, Maxisport,
23, Olga Besnard, 6, 7, 10, 21, Shooter Bob Square Lenses, cover,
throughout, Syda Productions, 9, testing, cover, 12, 19

Design elements: Shutterstock

Printed and bound in Canada.
010395F17

Table of Contents

Ballroom Dancing on Ice

Have you ever watched a celebrity dance series on TV? Making graceful moves, dance partners glide across the floor. Ice dancing has been described as ballroom dancing on ice. It focuses on footwork and how skaters move to music. It also requires great strength and athletic ability.

SAFETY FIRST!

If you want to try ice dancing, make sure you only practice moves when your coach or trainer is with you.

Fast Fact

In **international** events, ice dancing is performed by couples. But individuals can compete nationally.

Ice dancers work hard to make their routines look effortless.

History of Skating

Skating first began thousands of years ago. People in the Netherlands used to strap animal bones to their shoes so they could travel on frozen canals. Skating then spread to Britain, and figure skating clubs were set up. American Jackson Haines was the skater who brought a dance style to skating in the mid-1800s.

international—between or among the nations of the world

Chapter 1

Practice Makes Perfect

Most ice dancers start out in group lessons. If you reach a level where you are good enough to enter competitions, it is time to get an individual coach. Make sure you do some research before choosing one.

Things to consider include:

- Has the coach trained other successful ice dancers?

- Will the coach be able to help you find an ice dancing partner?

- Can the coach help you with **choreography**, choosing music, and costumes?

Coaches give skaters advice at competitions.

FINDING A PARTNER

While it is possible to ice dance alone, most people prefer to dance with a partner. Partners can often be found through your coach. You also may be able to find someone in your ice dance class or at your local skating club.

Partners train in costume for a big event.

TEST LEVELS

In ice dancing, there are test levels. These go from pre-juvenile to juvenile, intermediate, novice, junior, and finally senior. Senior is the level you see at the Olympics and World Championships. In order to move up a level, you must pass a test in front of judges.

choreography—the arrangement of steps, movements, and required elements that make up an ice dance routine

WORKING OFF ICE

The only way to improve your ice dancing skills is to keep practicing. Many senior-level ice dancers practice for more than 30 hours a week.

Improving your strength and **stamina** off the ice also helps to improve your performance on it. Pilates is a type of exercise that focuses on balance and strength. It is a popular way of training the **core**, which needs to be strong for skating. Many skaters also go to ballet classes.

Ballet helps to strengthen the body and improve balance. It also helps ice skaters become more **flexibile**.

Stamina comes from doing cardio exercises as well as strength training. Cardio exercise includes activities that raise your heart rate and make you breathe faster.

Benefits of Ice Dancing

There are many benefits to ice dancing: stronger legs, better balance, and improved flexibility. It even boosts brain power. Learning the choreography requires concentration and a good memory. Making sure you cover all the ice with your routine leads to better **spatial awareness**.

stamina—the ability to carry on doing an activity for a long time
core—muscles that control the lower back and tummy
flexible—able to bend or move easily
spatial awareness—being aware of the space around you

Chapter 2

Skills

Every skater needs to learn the basics. Ice dancing also requires skaters to perform certain lifts, spins, and step sequences.

LIFTS

The golden rule for ice dancers is that the woman cannot be lifted above the man's head. Instead, ice dancers can attempt **pull-throughs** and hand-to-hand hold lifts. Lifts can be done on the spot, while rotating, or while travelling in a straight line or a curve across the ice. Combination lifts involve putting two short lifts together.

An ice dancing team performs a rotational lift.

Skaters usually work with their coaches to choreograph the lifts in a studio. Ideas can come from many places, including acrobatics and TV dance shows. Skaters often first practice the lifts on the ground while wearing tennis shoes. Then they might progress to wearing skates but remain on the ground. The woman may wear a helmet too, just to be safe. Even when skaters move onto the ice, they take things slowly. The man keeps both feet on the ice and only adds rotations one at a time. Finally, the team adds speed.

Fast Fact

Sometimes the woman gets to lift the man! Several couples were known for performing reverse lifts, including British skaters John and Sinead Kerr (right).

pull-through—where one partner pulls the other under his or her legs

TWIZZLES

A twizzle is a one-foot turn while moving across the ice. The turns should be continuous but can change direction. The couple must perform **synchronized** twizzles. This means they must be performed at exactly the same time.

SPINS

Unlike twizzles, spins are done in one place on the ice. Each person can be in a different position during a dance spin, but they must perform it together in a dance hold. The couple must rotate at least three times in a dance spin.

STEP SEQUENCES

Step sequences are a set of steps in a **pattern dance**. They can also be the steps, turns, and movements that make up any ice dance routine. These include steps such as choctaw, mohawk, three turn, bracket, and rocker. Ice dancers do steps while skating in various positions and in different holds. The couple is allowed to separate for no longer than five seconds. Step sequences can be done in a straight line, in a curved line, in a circle, or diagonally.

Ice dancing involves some fancy footwork.

synchronized—together at the same time

pattern dance—steps, direction, and edges are shown in a diagram, which must be followed as closely as possible

Chapter 3

Rules and Scoring

For major events, the International Skating Union (ISU) decides which dance style will be the focus of the short dance. The ISU also sets out which **required elements** must be performed for both the short and the free dance.

Skaters perform in a free dance competition.

The International Skating Union

By the late 1800s, various styles of skating existed. For skaters to be judged fairly, the style of figure skating had to be the same for everyone. So the ISU was set up in 1892 to control the sport of skating worldwide. It set up rules for international figure skating competitions. The ISU now has about 70 member countries.

required element—particular move in skating that has to be included in a competition or test routine

SHORT DANCE

The short dance includes set ballroom and dance styles, such as blues or foxtrot, which change every year. The Senior level short dance must last for 2 minutes and 50 seconds, give or take 10 seconds. Required elements are chosen each year from the following:

- dance lift(s)
- dance spin(s)
- step sequence(s)
- set(s) of twizzles
- pattern dance element(s)
- choreographic element (no more than one)

FREE DANCE

In the free dance, skaters choose their own music and routine. The routine must include new dance steps and movements but also some required elements. The Senior-level free dance must last for 4 minutes, give or take 10 seconds. Required elements are chosen each year from the following:

- dance lift(s)
- dance spin(s)
- step sequence(s)
- set(s) of twizzles that are synchronized
- choreographic element(s), such as an extra spin or twizzle

SCORING

The International Judging System is used to score skaters' performances. It was set up in 2004 after controversy in the pairs competition at the 2002 Winter Olympics.

There are three to nine judges at competitions. Skaters are judged on how good their own performance is. They are not compared to other skaters. Each element of a routine is given a base value from the start. Judges then give each element a grade of execution (GOE), marking the quality of the element. The base value and the GOE of all elements add up to the technical score.

Judges watch closely as skaters perform their routines.

There is also a presentation score. Skaters are judged on skating skills, **transitions**, performance, and **composition**. They are judged on interpretation of the music and timing too. Interpretation is the meaning behind the music. The highest mark given for each is 10.

The skaters' total score is the technical score plus the presentation score minus any points taken off for any falls or for moves that are not allowed.

Scoring Controversy

In the 2002 Winter Olympics, Canadian pairs skaters Jamie Salé and David Pelletier skated almost perfectly. Russian pair Yelena Berezhnaya and Anton Sikharulidze made a mistake. Yet it was the Russians who won gold. After a complaint from Skate Canada, both pairs were given gold medals. The French judge later said she had been pressured into giving the Russians a higher mark in return for the French receiving a better mark in ice dancing.

Yelena Berezhnaya and Anton Sikharulidze (both in red) with Jamie Salé and David Pelletier

transitions—steps and movements that link the required elements in a routine

composition—the arrangement of movements in an ice dance routine, including how much of the ice is covered and how original it is

Chapter 4

Preparing for Competitions

Competitions give skaters a goal for which to shoot. They encourage skaters to train harder, improve their skills, and perform better. Preparation is important.

CHOOSING MUSIC

Choosing music to skate to is important in ice dancing. Performing to the beat of the music and interpreting it is central to scoring. Skaters have to feel comfortable with the music they choose. After all, they will be skating to it day in and day out.

Fast Fact

How about some heavy metal ice dancing? Estonian skaters Taavi Rand and Irina Shtork skated to Metallica's "Nothing Else Matters" in 2010.

Ice dancers' expressions should match the mood of the music as well.

CHOREOGRAPHY

Choreography has to match the type of music chosen by skaters. It also has to follow the ISU rules. If it doesn't, points can be lost when it comes to competition time. Ice dancers have to make sure that their routine matches the speed, rhythm, and mood of the music chosen.

19

COSTUMES

Costumes should also match the type of music chosen. They should not distract the audience or judges from the skating performance. Some skaters make their own costumes. Others ask designers to create outfits for them.

Christina and William Beier

Different fabrics create various effects. Small pieces of material flowing from a costume can suggest speed. Sometimes skaters' costumes are covered in sequins and crystals. These catch the light as ice dancers skate around the rink.

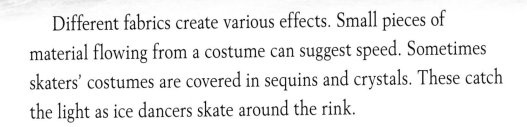

Fast Fact

Canadian Olympic gold medalist Tessa Virtue always has a safety pin on her costume. She believes it brings her good luck.

Tessa Virtue and Scott Moir

Chapter 5

Major Events

There are two major international events for the top skaters: the Winter Olympics and the World Championships. But there are many other competitions too. For these events, skaters must have met certain scoring goals at international competitions in the previous year. Each season the minimum score is decided by the ISU.

GRAND PRIX COMPETITIONS

The Grand Prix series of competitions includes junior and senior tournaments. There are six qualifying events each year. Those with the top scores compete in a final event. The finals of the junior competition and the senior competition are held at the same time.

OTHER COMPETITIONS

National competitions allow each country's best skaters to compete against one another. Included in the U.S. national competition program is the National Solo Dance Championships. This event allows individuals to ice dance competitively.

The Four Continents is a competition held every year for non-European countries. It first took place in 1999. Skaters must be at least 15 years old to compete.

Anna Yanovskaya
and Sergey Mozgov
at a Grand Prix
Competition

WORLD FIGURE SKATING CHAMPIONSHIPS

Ice dancing became part of the World Figure Skating Championships in 1952. The championships take place every year. Each country can send at least one ice dance team.

Marina Anissina and Gwendal Peizerat compete in the 1999 World Figure Skating Champinships in Finland.

Russians on Top

From 1980 to 2000, the Russians won the majority of World Championship ice dancing competitions. British skaters Jayne Torvill and Christopher Dean won their last World Championship in 1984. Marina Anissina and Gwendal Peizerat of France won in 2000. In between, only French ice dancers Isabelle and Paul Duchesnay could beat the Russians. They were world champions in 1991.

WINTER OLYMPICS

The Winter Olympics takes place every four years. Originally, Olympic figure skating did not include ice dancing. Ice dancing was finally accepted as an Olympic sport in 1976. Ice dancers must be 15 or older to compete. They qualify through a points system based on previous World Championships or placing at an international qualification event.

Fast Fact

Jean Westwood and Lawrence Demmy of Great Britain were named ice dancing's first world champions in 1952. The first Olympic ice dancing champions were Lyudmila Pakhomova and Aleksandr Gorshkov of the Soviet Union in 1976.

Lyudmila Pakhomova and Aleksandr Gorshkov

Chapter 6

Stars and Legends

Ice dancing stars perform ground-breaking routines and ever more athletic lifts. They have been inspirations to new skaters.

MERYL DAVIS AND CHARLIE WHITE

Meryl Davis was 9 and Charlie White was about 10 when they first started skating together. They won a bronze medal at the Junior World Championships. The couple won gold at the 2011 and 2013 World Championships. Their biggest success was winning the gold medal at the 2014 Olympics in Sochi.

Davis and White were the first ice dancers from the United States to win gold at the Olympics. Davis suggested that it was just the start of American ice dancing success.

Fast Fact

Meryl Davis was a bridesmaid at Charlie White's wedding in 2015.

Meryl Davis and
Charlie White

OKSANA GRISHUK AND EVGENI PLATOV

Russians Oksana Grishuk and Evgeni Platov became ice dance partners in 1990. In 1994 they won their first Olympic gold medal and followed it up with a World Championship. In 1994 they moved to Delaware so they could use better training facilities. The couple won more than 20 competitions in a row, including another Olympic gold in 1998. Grishuk and Platov are the only ice dancers to win Olympic gold twice.

Oksana Grishuk and Evgeni Platov

TESSA VIRTUE AND SCOTT MOIR

Canadians Tessa Virtue and Scott Moir began to skate together in junior competitions in 1998. They earned their first Junior Worlds medal in 2005. Three years later they were winning medals in the World Championships. They have won six World Championship medals, including gold in 2010 and 2012.

Virtue and Moir were the first North Americans to win an Olympic ice dance gold medal in 2010. Their rivalry with Meryl Davis and Charlie White, their training partners, dominated ice dancing from 2010 to 2014.

Tessa Virtue and Scott Moir

Glossary

canal (kuh-NAL)—human-made waterway used to get from one place to another

choreography (kor-ee-OG-ruh-fee)—the arrangement of steps, movements, and required elements that make up an ice dance routine

composition (KOM-poh-zi-shuhn)—the arrangement of movements in an ice dance routine, including how much of the ice is covered and how original it is

controversy (KAHN-troh-ver-see)—a public disagreement about something

core (KOR)—muscles that control the lower back and tummy

flexible (FLEK-suh-buhl)—able to bend or move easily

international (in-tur-NASH-uh-nuhl)—between or among the nations of the world

pattern dance (PAT-urn DANSS)—steps, direction, and edges are shown in a diagram, which must be followed as closely as possible

pull-through (PUL-throo)—where one partner pulls the other through his or her legs

required element (ri-KWY-urd EL-uh-muhnt)—particular move in skating that has to be included in a competition or test routine

spatial awareness (SPAY-shuhl uh-WAYR-nuhs)—being aware of the space around you

stamina (STAM-uh-nuh)—the ability to carry on doing an activity for a long time

synchronized (SING-kruh-nyzd)—together at the same time

transitions (tran-ZISH-uhnz)—steps and movements that link the required elements in a routine

Read More

Barnas, Jo-Ann. *Great Moments in Olympic Skating.* Great Moments in Olympic Sports. Minneapolis: SportZone, 2015.

Hunter, Nick. *The Winter Olympics.* Chicago: Heinemann Library, 2014.

Throp, Claire. *Figure Skating.* Winter Sports. Chicago: Raintree, 2014.

Internet Sites

Use FactHound to find Internet sites related to this book.

Visit *www.facthound.com*

Just type in 9781515781851 and go.

 Check out projects, games and lots more at
www.capstonekids.com

Index